Word Simple

Word Simple

HAROLD J. RECINOS

RESOURCE *Publications* • Eugene, Oregon

WORD SIMPLE

Copyright © 2017 Harold J. Recinos. All rights reserved. Except for brief quotations in critical publications or reviews, no part of this book may be reproduced in any manner without prior written permission from the publisher. Write: Permissions, Wipf and Stock Publishers, 199 W. 8th Ave., Suite 3, Eugene, OR 97401.

Resource Publications
An Imprint of Wipf and Stock Publishers
199 W. 8th Ave., Suite 3
Eugene, OR 97401

www.wipfandstock.com

PAPERBACK ISBN: 978-1-5326-1947-2
HARDCOVER ISBN: 978-1-4982-4575-3
EBOOK ISBN: 978-1-4982-4574-6

Manufactured in the U.S.A.   MAY 31, 2017

Contents

Look | 1
Shout | 2
Apologize | 3
Other Shores | 4
Say | 5
The Place | 6
Night | 7
Old Revolutionaries | 8
The Walk | 10
The Shadows | 11
Redemption | 12
Salsa Night | 13
The Future | 14
Passages | 15
Unshaken | 16
Cold Day | 17
Believe | 18
The Wall | 19
Been Gone | 20
Follow Me | 22

Rising Up | 24
The Stripper | 25
Charmed | 26
The Apartment Visit | 27
The Girl | 29
I, Believe | 30
Rock Bread | 31
Becoming | 32
Stand Up | 33
Silence | 34
The Move | 35
Presidential Debate | 37
The Hallway | 38
Face Paint | 40
The Playground | 41
The Workers | 42
Trying Times | 43
Leaked | 44
Panchimalco | 45
Subway | 46

Contents

The Box | 47
First Prayer | 48
The Wait | 49
Trump Up | 51
The Knot | 52
Laurence | 53
The Vision | 54
Struggle | 56
The Garden | 57
The Nameless | 58
Starry Night | 59
Halloween Night | 60
Stick Ball | 61
There is Time | 62
Tenderness | 63
Wonder | 64
Election Day | 65
The Poor | 66
The Day After | 67
The Stone | 68
Kindness | 69
Evening Prayer | 70
Election Day | 71
Imagine | 72
Letter to my Brother | 74
Poverty | 76
The Birth | 77
Thanksgiving Day | 78
Got It | 80
Hudson Hotel | 82

Wings | 84
Fordham Road | 85
Old Church | 86
Answer | 87
Waiting | 88
Bend | 89
The Pier | 90
Ponder | 91
El Barrio | 92
Simple | 93
The Big Tree | 95
Here | 96
Christmas, Rockefeller Center | 97
Redemption | 99
Piety | 100
The Musician | 101
Peace | 102
The Drop | 103
The Guitar | 104
False Arrest | 105
The Mother | 107
New Year | 108
After School | 109
Where | 110
Cold | 111
¡Ay, Bendito! | 112
Lost Day | 113
Rain | 114
Flight | 115
The Climb | 117

Contents

Sound | 118

The Way | 119

The Stand | 120

Knock | 121

Hunts Point | 122

Exit | 123

Lament | 124

Awake | 125

This time | 126

Lent | 127

Roadside | 128

Beloved Community | 129

What Matters | 130

Bread | 131

Simple Wood | 132

Fish Platter | 133

The Other Side | 135

Pouring Rain | 137

The Boys | 138

The Stoop | 139

Say! | 140

Graduation | 141

Clothesline | 142

Bus Ride | 143

Mr. President | 145

LOOK

look,
at me from
where you
live,
laborer, cook,
dishwasher, housekeeper,
nanny, cashier,
janitor, trucker,
farm hand, brick layer,
carpenter, and retail clerk.
tell me you know
our Spanish tears,
the noise
they make,
and the
insolvency we
hardly ever
escape.
look at me
in the day's
tired hours,
leaning against
the wall
on the corner,
waiting to
sit with
you
to talk
of things.

SHOUT

I imagine there are a thousand
ways to pour discouragement

out, to see light rise from ashes,
or find the other side of sadness

come up from watering eyes. when
I went up to ring the church bells,

to scare the nighttime ghosts down
the grieving streets, far from the

two old men sobbing, beyond the
aged cemetery now covered with

lilies, and past the piteous hearts
of children with hope turned to

dust, I wondered about the best
way to wrestle with this world

that prohibits us? surely, there are
a thousand ways to end these days

keeping us thirsty, hungry, hardened,
and afraid. if you come close take hold

of our hands, the dreams we make, and
have a look at the blood and bones that

moves when called by name. at
midnight, dash to the rooftop with

us to shout, enough!

APOLOGIZE

what time are the politicians
coming back to apologize for
ignoring the transparent truth,
the whimpering on the streets,
the apartments full of corpses
leaving behind a landslide of
grief? when will they shiver
in our imprisoned cold, kneel
with the martyrs of the Bethlehem
star, and sit on the stoops in the
August heat? I worry they have
not learned to say the right things,
spend their time boiling our tears,
and work in deep sleep. today, I
plan to send these letters written by the
dead that are full of sentences to make
them simply see!

OTHER SHORES

those voices you do not hear,
faceless through all the years,

beaten down by batons, political
speech, angry cold stares, left

with festering wounds on the
filthy streets are newcomers here

who pushed from your dreams
mirror a overlooked history. the

grieving maids in your homes, the
gardeners who help your flowers

grow, the brick layers putting up
the fancy neighborhood mansions,

the wounded who sob emptying
the rubbish bins in the offices that

make this country rich, the children
who long for their deported parents

from unimaginable depths are like
you in the settling night searching

simply for a place to call sweet, sweet
home. in the ordinary days when you

cannot find time to listen to the words
shouting of another world, when you

turn away from dark hands that offer to
set you free, in the silences across

this earth, the revelations of detested
refugees, remember these lives and

all their other tongues more than the
management's present inhumanity.

SAY

the children
cry justice
beneath
heaven's
dimming light,
a thing in
cruelty past
so many did
see. the older
generation with
near forgotten
dreams reaches
with the darkest
hands
for signs
that read
Lord of Mercy,
tell these
people
full of
hate, America,
the beautiful,
so beautiful
too with me.

THE PLACE

they read the English clocks made
in China, always go to work on time,

play the lottery for a big hit, never complain
of a thing, walk the unknown streets, send their

kids to schools offering books with a hundred pages
missing, bury their dead in cheap wood with grief

fixed to their wrinkled faces, breathe the angry air
telling them how to misspell their names, live to

see poverty abounding from generation to the
next, know hunger, illness, fatigue, work that keeps

them close to death, and listen to the devilish cries
of hate that surrounds them in a forgotten place so

carefully slighted by all your Gods. they lean into
the light of day, stand in the quiet of night, kneel

in prayer in sparsely furnished rooms, talk
with ghostly listeners, and wait for an answer to

their cries from a world unwilling to deliver even
a hint of slanting light. when the children ask what

dreams will come for them, what will you whisper
into their beautiful innocent ears?

NIGHT

every night she sat
at the kitchen table

eating bread, her old age
telling me not to close

the door, and listen to her
closely for truth. she was

like a book checked out of
an old library before my eyes

with a soul deeper than a
city beggar's cup. we sat

quietly at the table listening
to the wind howl outside the

window, the radiator talking in
the cold space like it was reading

a Charles Dickens' novel. then,
in silence beyond help, the elderly

woman told me she dreamed her
teen son alive again in the apartment

saying to her, "mother." I remember
that night so clearly, we looked at old

photographs that adored hearing her
speak, images frozen in time, with

sounds of crying and laughter roaming
in the old ladies heart. that night, I

pleaded to God above let this woman
know sweet love and everlasting

peace.

OLD REVOLUTIONARIES

there is a place for times like this
where old revolutionaries thought

gone still gather to talk about how
they overcame persecuting days in

another country. for decades they
have roamed our city streets in the

shadows quietly observing how the
truth that helped make them more

human is so carefully crushed now
by an authoritarian flattery that has

seduced the nation to a culture of
threat with well-placed lies ready

to violently pounce on the innocent
without consequence. I sat on the

stoop with these old rebels wondering
out loud with them what it would mean

to live unafraid from those you have
called your own? last night with these

old friends, I opened the Bible searching
with a flashlight for a few lines to speak

to our times only to find pages full of words
that pulled back all the blinds and questioned

the piety of this season of hate. these old
insurrectionists who have lived for so long

among those who want to do them in,
still say in this haunted world a new

day will come—so I will remain with them
measuring each day with the intelligence that

offers generous lasting change.

THE WALK

let us walk beneath the
half-moon sky in search

of deserted streets, to the
little park on the other side

of Southern Boulevard, the
grandmothers love to visit

to mutter prayers and talk
of everything. let us sit on

a bench to watch the cross
town bus makes it way down

the block with passengers riding
sideways wearing faces wrinkled

by years of trouble, then throw
bread at the unruly pigeons, and

talk with Hank the wino who
after a pint of Midnight Express

recites lines written by the lonely
men who live under the bridge.

let us open our ill at ease eyes to
see the things here that are hardly

understood, the broken windows
of tenements, the gutted cars on

the streets, the children who play
in shortened years, the furnished

rooms with hearts stretched sad,
the rubble of the empty lots, and

congas pounding fatalistic beats
at the Ortiz Funeral home. let us

walk all night long until we find
a drop of twisted light to dry our

damp souls and to rattle us to the
very bottom of our feet.

THE SHADOWS

have we come all this way to
live in the shadow of daily
threat, to stagger through the
days filling our eyes with all
worthwhile just out of reach,
to ponder while living what
will happen at the next work
place raid, the wordless message
our children will have to take to
bed, the useless insistence to the
powers in place that we too are
human beings? have we come
all this way to drown in tears
like crossers swallowed by the
river, to feel stabbing pain at
the sight of the big black cars
delivering us to graves, and the
doors of Hell left wide open just for
us? have we come this far to stand
just beyond the light, to listen to the
calls to prayer, tales of punishment,
the Holy Spirit sobbing, and friends
who say farewell? have we come this
far, floated rivers, walked desserts,
lived years with bent backs, beaten
spirits, stuttering tongues, just to see
our children's innocence so carefully
not spared? tell me America do you
still dream?

REDEMPTION

my old man sailed the ocean
on a big old ship owned by
Uncle Sam in a second world
war evil wished for a country
that today would not offer shelter
to the Guatemalan likes of him.
my old mother neither black or
white held petty-wage jobs longer
it seemed than her bitter life in a
country that only called her spic.
my old man died a veteran of
a foreign war for a country never
home, freedom not ever his, and
that fine White House not taking
calls now from people with dark
skin. my old mother died nearly
alone in a convalescent home, crying
the nurses said every night to get
hell out, hearing the scratchy
sounds of her first born son laid
for final rest too young in a Staten
Island grave, alone. I see them
clearly in my slice of the world,
pray forgiveness for cursing them,
plead their cause present in the faces
of new immigrants, terrified refugees,
Black, Red, Yellow and poor White
lives. they told me one day a long box
would fall out of heaven to collect people
full of hate who dance around lynching
trees—I promised to do my part to hasten
the drop!

SALSA NIGHT

in the café the salsa band
charms the crowd, the eyes

are on the little man running
his stubby fingers over the keys

of an upright piano, trombones
slide notes to the corners of the

room, two trumpets have a long
conversation with the congas still

showing a tiny overlooked price
tag dangling from a lug, and at a

table next to the bass player sit a pious
looking couple ready to write Psalms

on the dance floor. life everywhere
in the club can easily be seen through

the window facing the street, felt by
aching souls, bleeding feet, colorless

dreams, and the spinning high places
never seen. in the café the salsa players

offer oil for childish days, harmonies
that set us free, and songs that make us

glad to weep—come and see!

THE FUTURE

the future is the long sidewalk
with grandmothers pulling simple

wheeled grocery carts, kids playing
on the street, single mothers disappearing

in church, and Nuyorican youth trying
hard to please the old Irish priest's God.

the future is quietly kneeling in the dark,
praying for fathers to hold their liquor each

Friday night, waking up for another day of
school, and leaving the classroom not saying

that sucked. the future is reaching for the
ones who are gone like a miracle crawling

from the flower garden on the empty lot
of the block with its own procession of

house birds. the future is a matter
of Spanish shouting in tongues, Angels

loudly clapping, time without so much
public strife, and the precious browning

of these streets. the future in a drop of
light, shows our lovely colored faces

on this block where nations meet—so I'll
sit a little longer on this stoop watching

a new world spinning into shape.

PASSAGES

one by one the memories
stored the length of many
years rise in unexpected

places to walk you back in
time and help you feel the
sustaining mystery of each

simple day. you laugh alone
on a favorite park bench lost
in dreamy things in a body

pushing an age each week
more tattered than the favorite
book you carry to page in the

caressing wind. you look up
at the heavens wondering what
the sky looked like the day you

were born, who told stories of
the distant moon and stars, the
feeling of that first night with

breath. you recall playing on
the streets, the first time you
delighted touching brown earth,

and seeing childish things you
still dream to glimpse. in more
than a thousand ways your brittle

bones want to shout all around
I live glorious in interior might,
with soul too deep for sight, and

drenched with the blessings of
falling stars. I promise, whenever
you gaze upward, I too will take a

a look at the great mystery always
making your wrinkled face smile
without end.

UNSHAKEN

we are not
shaken no
matter how the
day is
split in two by
raids conducted
in the name of
the pathetic vanity
of a White House
that goes to
lengthy ends
to convince us all to
hate.
the liberating light
coming from
above
does even now
lift the threatening
grime tossed from
the filthy lips
souring our State
rooms.
we are not shaken
by the senile
blame,
the scolding that
roams
along the Southern border,
echoes in our
homes,
and
bounces against
open
church doors.

we are not shaken,
by all the curses
the men of
single breed
conceive to
sire everything
unwanted by
America's most
deep-hearted
dream.

COLD DAY

the first cold days in the early
morning hinting winter, leaves
twirling around in the chilly air,
the sun now a cool distant friend,
a walk in the woods not knowing
the names of trees, down a winding
path where there are no questions, to
places never seen, birds that will show
up tonight to rest on the city lampposts
performing gracious flight and wordless
songs. a bark far off on the other side of
the woods for no reason breaks the silence
like the blades of grass pushing up without
warning on cracked sidewalks. the time
of day no longer matters, the name of things
a reminisced convention, inhaling with each
step the scent of the air, reaching the banks
of the slow river, resting with no regret in
the company of the tide that gently scratches
its back on the shore—a lumbering truth waits
here!

BELIEVE

there
is a land of
make believe
in a place
not everyone
can fit,
where
you never sleep,
and time is ever so
slowly
spent dreaming
of things.
everyone
who visits it
comes back
to the block full
of all kinds of tales
like Angels surrounded
by the universe
squeezed into a field
made from crown-rimmed
bottle caps, and
raised Lazarus
doing Simpson Street
raps to put
listeners in love
with
God.
people,
talk there
with lips that never
move but
you can plainly
hear them, and
they swear
the poor are
never
overlooked
and
all the
Spanish speaking
junkies are
cured.

THE WALL

there
was a time in
history
that never
loved a wall,
the fear
that builds
it tall,
the gloom
it so pretends,
the weeping
on the other side
unheard by those
who sleep.
there
was a time in
history
that could not
tolerate the hand-made
bricks laid on quiet
earth
convening
mindless hate
that falls like
hail from the
darkest sky
to make compassion
bleed.
there
was a time in
history
that dared not
imagine
the border
snapped shut
by a president
who never groaned
with guilt for
God.
there
was a time in
history
that
rejected all
goose-stepping
dreams.
rejoice,
there
will be a time
when
heaven's
trumpets will
sound
to tumble
the wall
and
the fool
of all these
thing.

BEEN GONE

spent a whole lot of years gone
from here, disappeared in a pale

world that never gave a welcome
mat to people like me, and out

of pure spite leveled point-blank
hate my way. walked in too many

places that turned from created human
beings that wanted to secure sinister

damnation for the brown skinned poor,
lowly, excluded, left out and fucked up.

knocked on a whole lot of doors never
opened, lived the innocent years pursued

by unmentionable fear, the relentless odor
of death, and condemning threats from a white

world with dark seeping in its heart. closed
my eyes with every step, lined up in a few

special places for bread, listened to the old
women on the block with shrinking spines

tell me don't give up, and carried the kindness
of Julia, Sonia, Joseph, Rudy, Tito, Carmen,

Tony, Shorty and Lefty now become
names on a block wall. spent a whole lot of

years gone from here, never forgetting to
scream for the tiny bones we buried and

the people the world refuses to see that
are so sweetly mine!

FOLLOW ME

if you would walk with me
down this wide street into

another world, the people who
know how to prowl in the darkness,

who speak outright in the daylight,
and take God with them, will greet

you with smiles bright like flames. you'll
be surprised to know they have been

looking for you, since the night an
old Brown lady yelled in the storefront

church on the corner *gloria a Dios* change
is coming, soon. if you like, we can stop

in to see this old woman who knows how
to pull apart the gods people have carefully

made, she will listen to the stories you
care to conjure, and then she will tell you

to face the closed door her children have
pounded for years. if you walk with me

a little further, to the bodega where the old
men once soldiers sit, you will discover from

them the stains on our democracy were
made with blood and all kinds of colored

skin. you may be surprised, by the close
of this stroll beneath the fat moon, you

may end up talking with new depth
into our light and dreams.

RISING UP

    quietly,
    I sat in the rising
    light of this day absorbed
    by news of a new president
    who hardly gives a thought
    to a future of peace, the people
    who sing their children to sleep in
    Spanish, the blameless refugees who
    recall with prayer the God who lives
    in the Middle East, the shouting eyes
    of women marching the streets, and
    the Black lives rising up to chase away
    darkness from every side.

    quietly,
    I listened to the chirping birds around me
    say in their very gentle ways, the great
    Maker filled the lot of us with life to rob
    the moron in power a lengthy Oval Office
    stay, their songs filled me with the most
    peculiar joy for in the faces of all those the
    bellicose leader scorns with his indecorous
    rhetoric of hate the richer light of the One
    crowned with thorns staggers from the dark
    to make a loving case.

    quietly,
    I recollected while pushing hope into the
    tormented day, the new White House clay
    will one day also turn to dust, have to reckon
    with the angry breathe of God, and wonder
    on the road to Peter's Gate past the great
    hills folding above the life settled from sea
    to shining sea what awaits him—I chuckled
    at the thought: A Wall!

THE STRIPPER

one night
in the middle of winter
moonlight flooded
the bedroom
to make it
feel a world
without end.
But looking
out the window
at the strained street,
I recalled
the smell of the
bar where Sonia
dissolved
dreams
dancing near
naked for greasy
men who
emptied their pockets
of change for a
peak.
my heart twisted
remembering
the day Sonia
said Johnny the
cop wanted her
to be his
perfect girl.
I cried recalling
the walk in the
little park where
Sonia stepped on a dry leaf
that crunched so loudly
beneath her foot she
whispered—that is
life for me. I looked
up at the moon with
my wet eyes stared
it in the face to say Sonia
with her choked heart
is trying to outlast
these splitting
days.

CHARMED

she sits in a rocking chair going
back to the stories that charmed

her heart for hours, tales read in
the dim light of a child's room

that shaped excitement with the
simple turn of a page, heroines

met in the woods, Cinderella losing
a shoe, God walking in garden, a

Pegasus in the sky pushing cotton
ball clouds, journeys to the bottom

of the sea, young boys chasing down
glory, and clocks with blind delight

relaxing the forward march of time.
in her aged imagination the entire world

is no more than a miniature country, a
lonely dwelling, the fading earth, a thing

meant to be vaguely understood. the seasons
speak to her now in long sentences that last

well into the night, they forget sometimes
to smile at her, but unafraid of all this change

the old woman simply waits for the future
always in the quiet room reaching for simple

plans and the warmth of light.

THE APARTMENT VISIT

the last time I visited Carmen
she said the neighbors upstairs
are stealing her mail. some nights

she imagines they are standing just
outside her apartment door casting
spells to turn her hours into ice cold

stone. when you walk by her door
on the third floor of the building it's
easy to hear her talking to her dead

son about the days they use to go out
dancing in the Bronx clubs Tito Puente
played, the aluminum Christmas tree

they would put up each year with a
rainbow colored spot light shining in
a dark living room on it, the trips to

Orchard Beach to stand looking over
the sound talking about how to rope
the waves to walk them back to the

apartment on the block, and the light
bulb in the closet not changed since
the day he passed away. for every corner

of the block, she has stories to tell to make
you see Jesus standing knee deep in the river
where John poured a whole bunch of water

over the unemployed carpenter's head. the
night I stopped to visit with a bag of groceries,
Carmen asked me to sit down to talk about

her long trip to light candles at the church, then
dreaming that night of flying over the rooftops
coated with Puerto Rican flags to keep them

warm, pass the little creek where little
Sonia drowned, over the little league baseball
fields where her son played, and back to the

two room apartment. Can you tell me what it
means? I remember the kitchen radio playing
Celia Cruz singing, *Te Busco,* not knowing what

to say. wanting to sell my tongue for being
speechless, I leaned over the table, and gently
kissed the old women on her beautifully wrinkled

cheek.

THE GIRL

On Saint Mark's Place, the girl
in the coffee shop has been there
wearing out since young. nearing
late middle age without sadness,
she is never bothered by the kids
who use the next door wall to thump
a game of handball. when her mother
died last year she moved about slowly,
cried in transit between tables, and
spoke for several weeks with words
featuring single syllables. the spent
years have buried themselves not to be
heard from again on this street and slowly
the old who greeted her in the morning are
also turning away in dust. the girl in the coffee
shop no longer queen of the high school prom
is turning gray, and though she needs
to rest now to draw sweet breath, I always
clearly see in her a world within the world,
sweet innocence full of light the dark will
never win.

I, BELIEVE

I believe in a world of goodness
that can be seen in plain daylight,

sometimes by just looking around
with ears closed to the noises of

ignorance and hate, you can see it
rolling from the five story tenements

like a huge boulder falling from the
sky with children at play on it, in

the faces leaning out the windows
calling for the future to hurry up with

good news, in the sounds of delicious
Salsa pouring from the front door of

the barbershop where the old men
who came from the island too many

years ago linger with near bald
heads to laugh, in the local library

around the corner where junior high
school kids hang out after school to

discover things to love in English
like Melville, Twain, Ellison,

Hughes, Anaya, Castillo, among
centuries of carefully tended books.

I believe in days filled with wonder,
the almighty hanging around in the

thickest dark, born a foreigner in
these parts, building a big old

outhouse for twisted politicians
with lying tongues that like to

keep us down.

ROCK BREAD

I have to tell you loud
do not eat this hard rock
bread tossed to us from
the White House. It will
not nourish a single drop
of our dreams, give life
to Black hands, feed Brown
skin, or give any sister a
taste of influence. I have to
tell you loud today do not
eat the rock hard bread tossed
from a window on that capital city
street by a man who laughs around
the dinner table with friends quite
fond of lynching trees. I have to
tell you loud scream from all the
rooftops with the weight of past
sorrows and the thickest blood of
freedom: *America in her luxurious
diversity shall rise above these bitter
times yet again to dream!*

BECOMING

in the long unwritten history of this
block becoming, its future spreading

through the forgotten bodies stretching
arms through the heavens to feel for

God dwelling somewhere in love, the
cold city towers listening to our days

held in hand, beyond the time when
rainbows pranced around in thick upstairs

clouds, we toss into the wind our sorrows,
hopes and dreams. in the places where

we sit invisible like the blade of grass in
a wide green field, with patient stares in

the fading light of day, we grieve the world
speechless of us. in the images flooding our

hearts, the words pouring from our lips that
lose their way by the time they reach uptown,

the sad walks to church old like the wind, the
vast sanity of the stars tempting us with mystery,

we dry the holy water dripping from our eyes, pray
without confusion, and ever so foolishly smile about

life held for us by the Ageless just-above that
so carefully leans to reach us.

STAND UP

a politician
who has read
is going to
leave office
for private citizenship
in an approaching
time of folly.
the sounds
of diminished life
can already be heard
from the elderly, women,
children, those named
a threat by the new
leader of some hateful
pale skins.
what the country
made from fear
will parade
in the
coming years
is an impersonated
democracy
for all the world to
see.
from beneath
the rocks the
hump-backed politicians
will arise to play
their role excusing
the white barbed wire
for the new fence, the
shots fired on the Black
and Brown kids, the civil
rights speakers to be set on fire,
and the stories of past greatness that
never mention the lynching trees.
in the face of recollected struggle,
I, a brown man, will stand with America's
great subversive dream: *government
for, by and of the people.*

SILENCE

some,
are told to be
silent,
to let their
protest
against injustice
remain
hunched
in the darkest
corners
where ancestors who
once generously
gave their
blood
now grunt
about tyrannies
to come from a
pale hand
of a politician
who will
offer a
maniacal smile
to those he hopes
to nail to quiet
country trees.
some,
are overcome
by an odd need
to pray to idols
made of
hate, to crowd
the cathedrals of
disbelief, and gleefully
shout when they
pierce colored
bodies like it was
done to the
brown man
crowned with
thorns.

THE MOVE

the car that breaks down every
three blocks is packed with five

carton boxes, a rocking chair,
two lamps, a coffee table, and

the altar Saints for the move just
around the corner. they will come

back for the kitchen and bed room
sets with the dark-faced children sound

asleep in their hearts, in the deep night
when the devil gathers junkies on the

block to march them to the infinite
abyss, alleyway cats will scurry about

with blood dripping from their teeth. the
family was driven to another cage by a

landlord with an ugly smile who came to say
spics get lost, sit in your Sunday mass to ask

for a new place to live, and move before the
white day is done. the car came back for

the apartment remains, the young mother
with sweet memories held in her arms stood

in the empty living room crying for America
the brave that does not look for her among the

heaps of wasted lives no promises keep. with
her lips trembling, she walked the apartment

rooms to say farewell to the blameless space
that even on the days God was too ill to hear

her pleas was nothing less than home.

PRESIDENTIAL DEBATE

where else can I look upon a screen
to see two restless politicians debate

the deepest meanings of the dawn's
early light, the burden of taxes, dreadful

economic slides, foes prowling silently
in the dark, and the flag in the victories

of tomorrow waved?   where else will I
see America singing precious visions

from her daughter's lips, or witness a
loud mouthed imbecile growing splinters

on his tongue?   where else can I see politics
beating on drums, bursting into living rooms,

and making promises of magnificent prosperity
and peace?   America, in this autumn beauty on

the wondrous debate floor, I saw the ancient
faces, the world on this land bleed, and a bit of

hope brightening the dark for us.

THE HALLWAY

one afternoon, when snow fell from the
sky big enough to shake alley clotheslines,

the neighborhood kids ready for a Spring
trip to a Jersey amusement park, bowed

their heads in a tenement hall to call
on *la virgen del Carmen* like the old

women who dusted the statue of the
Holy Mother in church. belief widened

their eyes, when they said in perfect broken
English *madrecita de Dios* even though the

weather has nothing to do with Saints, priests
or Mass, intervene. they were sick of being in

the hall, tired of the apartment doors opening
with elderly heads leaning for a look, hateful

of the shadows made by light bulbs dangling
above welfare collecting mailboxes that haunted

their need for a humble day of peace. a few of
the kids let tears fall to the floor, others cussed

the sadness they heard splash on it, and
together they objected having snow fall

on Easter Sunday. they longed to be in the
amusement park to see the new wax museum,

jump on rides, walk the latest house of ghosts,
and see pale faced people on the other side of

the George Washington bridge with small American
flags pinned to wrinkled shirts. they begged *la*

madrecita to walk them from the hallway,
away from that snowy day and to amusement park

salvation!

FACE PAINT

the noon bells ring with Autumn
voices letting us know it's time to

let Summer go to feel the wind that
rustles leaves in the sickly city trees. the

night offers now a touch of cold and the
moon is pushing across a sky full of stars

like a ghost visiting with the deepest secrets
to tell. it is time to make peace with fading

light, join the children who gallop toward
the jack-o'-lantern dark singing scary things,

toil, trouble, cauldron bubbles like the English
poet said. time to allow yellowing leaves to gently

touch chilly bones, and sit quietly in the
dark silence to count the ways we love the

laughing stoops of another Halloween.
we lean into this night of painted faces, bagged

treats, and frosty pumpkins carved for candle
lights, and tumble softly into the places these

trick-o-treating kids have touched to fill
our yearning hearts with their sweet and

gracious gifts.

THE PLAYGROUND

the sidewalk is the kids'
playground, where they

are in constant motion
at all ages without need

of swings, where the old
women patch scraped knees,

wipe watery eyes, and laugh
so loud at the girls who play

hopscotch, the pigeons on
the phone wires are startled

into flight. the sidewalk is a place
boys crash whirling tops like bumper

cars in circles drawn with chalk,
and garbage cans are used for

soccer games. in fire hydrants
open for play, kids find a hundred

ways to wet brown faces pouring
laughter on the hot streets, and in

front of their graffiti tenement walls
painted with the names of heroes and

the cherished words of dreams. the
sidewalk too is a playground where junkies

find religion in stores, and the elderly at
their open windows, see darkness sliced

to pieces by children as they play.

THE WORKERS

it's still dark outside and
the workers are sitting in
front of the locked warehouse
eating fresh bread with a side
of coffee. they are not saying
very much this early morning
just glad to enjoy the quiet before
the new work day starts. when
light begins to gently break into
the wide cloudless sky I can see
what makes each of them a labor
of elegant beauty. I sit with my
coffee beside them knowing the
moment will be worthy of mention
the whole day and my entire life
to come.

TRYING TIMES

with stoic calm, we watch them
talk about us with sharp tongues

rotting of hate and looks to frighten
the dead. with hearts about to burst,

we wonder what to call these times, the
reason for their threatening thoughts,

the screws come loose from our country's
dreams, in these days abounding with loss.

like scientist who say the whole damn
universe may one day fall into a black hole

to hasten the end, we sit in the shadows with
the terrifying thought this plunge will begin

with our flesh. we go to the altar to let our
weeping be seen, feeling sadness about so

much across this land that has slipped into
utter silence, America sweet land of liberty

with kind grace we beg you wake from this
foul sleep.

LEAKED

I turn to see the look in your
eyes coughed to the surface by

the leaked tape of a presidential
candidate with a lewd tongue on

his tower of Babel, falling. its late
at night, when the feeling of being

swept full of dirt inside raises the
question of what to do with a man

who lives to trap women beneath
his weight, with no praise for color

on his lips, and lynching trees for
any who disagree. we pause to

tell tales of guardian angels, river
crossings in the dark, children tracked

by dogs, the names of the places to hide,
and reaching the homes of old women who

heal in the North. you looked at me asking
how long in a Trump world until they

issue warrants for us, death sentences for
the faultless, beatings for broken English

dreams, and schools that teach only white
things? I cried beside you hoping the tears

would take your sadness long enough to see
God's gracious wind is even now blowing

the other way.

PANCHIMALCO

in the old church in the village
square old women come to visit

every day with their penance scarred
knees to clean dust from Saints carved

two centuries ago by people from a
distant Spanish shore. they gather at the

altar rail after the cleaning, scarves on
their Pipil heads, crossing themselves, and

deep in conversation with the Most High.
people on visit walk around them looking

at the paintings of Christ hanging on the walls
along the sanctuary aisles, staring at the Roman

Cross that has not moved for over two hundred
years, and taking pictures of the prayerful elders

whose truth is less interesting than having a native
face on film. these women gave their youth boarding

buses in front of the church bound for work in
wealthy homes, washing, cooking, taking care of

children and keeping house for families that could
not see creation in wrinkling Indian faces, divinity in

precious red skin, and life despite toil breathing
so free. I kneel before these elders from that old

village in the valley for they know how to look
at the world, and see.

SUBWAY

the subway is progressing
downtown full of workers

more familiar with cutting
sugar cane than pushing

coat racks along seventh
avenue. the train travels south

above ground past neon signs
with too many missing lights to

complete a single word, it then
plunges into the ground below

Manhattan streets. the pretty lady
sitting between two kids is singing

loud and keeping passengers around
her with tightly held breath for the

ride. one kid stares at a train rider standing
before him in paint stained clothes who

smiles, then the psychedelic painter lets
his eyes roam the crowded car looking for

signs to speak to his graying days water
coloring walls in a downtown factory. before

the next stop, darkness whispers in a tunnel,
and people look at each other conscious of

heading to the stations on the other side of
town that will feed on their aching lives.

THE BOX

the boy tried to put happiness in
a box only to discover with startled
interest the high wanderer of the block
would not stay. she climbed out of it
in the middle of the night, whispered
something in the boys ears, walked
past his tiny searching eyes, brushed
an invisible curtain aside, and jumped
out the fifth floor window to make the
rounds on the street below.   when the
boy rushed to the window to look out
happiness was kneeling in front of a very
crowded stoop with kids cracking jokes
to whom she offered a handful of flowers
grabbed from Lela's fire escape display on
the way down. the boy saw huge smiles
on the faces of friends out late that night who
no doubt liked the gift and thought divinity
of any kind should show up just like happiness,
rather than in shadows and bad dreams.

FIRST PRAYER

this morning after shaking the crumbs
from last night's tablecloth at the kitchen

window, she made her way into the altar
bedroom to offer up a few prayers to la *Virgen*

del Carmen whom she believed never spent
time thinking about applauding God, finding

light for walks in the dark, or figuring out for
the sake of her soul the little mysteries of life.

quietly, she kneeled a few moments before a
candle that burned for ceramic Saints, while

the curling flame twisted its way to her lips
to offer a round of words. she talked about used up

workers living in the building, dishwashers,
custodians, beauticians, barbers, lace-workers,

short-order cooks, men called shoe shine boys,
the slumped over from the calamity of underpaid

routines. she thought about the church over
on the far side of the block, Christ on a Cross

in a pitch black night waiting for a hand
with light, communion wafers that seldom

mean anything, and a God who likes overlooking
the block. then, she ended the morning prayer so

filled with complaint like this: Lord, remember
us!

THE WAIT

I was laying on a subway seat,
buried beneath a collection of

castoff Spanish language newspapers,
waiting for good news to walk

onto the train, to flood my thirteen
year old head with the words you

come back home. the walls of the
subway car wept for me, while I held

on for too many hours for anyone to
show beneath the stars, and the block's

cold graves, with these words of good
news. in oversized rags, I waited for the

matter to begin, my hands already reaching
to toss the old news print covering me. I

waited too for the one who walked across
the waters to board the IRT with a few

words of reassurance for a former altar
boy like me, to give evidence on the train

of love, and assure me silence was not his
best trick. I waited for his arrival like a church

steeple calmly holding a cross, but the talked
up Savior did not show. instead, some old guy

got on subway with a radio playing salsa tunes
featuring a trombone that made me dance. the

radio man stayed for two stops, the music
made me think of my two siblings whispering

their fears in a family so far from God.

TRUMP UP

the clown comes out with faded
colors to campaign for hours

with unhappy news of gloom
that is not true. perhaps by the

end of the election year, he will sit
down to contemplate a line from

the Russian writer who gave us
The Idiot to learn about the good

ways of open-hearted simplicity
that answers to the leaked light of

of those who cry in burning thickets
for mercy. the clown still tosses words

into space the air refuses to hold up
to the ears of those yet human who

slowly melt in his furnace. the clown
unable to sniff the scent of a wounded

year of boundless hate may soon need to
run like a fugitive into a thin night with

no exit. you see, those who wait for sounds
to be let loose from the sky will shout with

beloved Martin and everyone seared by
violence, hate and injustice *I have a dream,*

uncrushed!

THE KNOT

like a knot around the building
slowly tightening around those

forsaken by heaven, the writing
on its walls calling out names,

dreams and the relentless need for
rest, we wonder do others in this

city hear us holler. inside
no one tries to explain the knots

in the apartments with mothers
from conquered lands who are

punished by the violence on the
streets that beat and kill their

kids. in whispers, they wonder
who will announce an end to looking

into pits with the drying bones of
their sons and daughters, life darkening

souls, or say the Lord is no longer
too sick to work redemption on their

wretched streets. the knot is tight
around the words pouring from these

mothers' throats who imagine what
to say to those who nosily laugh with

indifference.

LAURENCE

I have heard it said that everything
is measured in the passage of time,
the mournful who see you in life's
destined end know this all too well.
though hearts beat together now like
hushed drums, I can tell you of the
smiles lined beside your coffin mindful
you were not made for dust. in the daily
strife, you made grace arise with a life
sublimely reaching others with God's
way of assessing things—so you often
told. these tears falling to earth help us
to toddle now toward the mysterious light
you adoringly taught in the charmed air
of too many rooms and places to count.
with bowed heads, we will continue to
stomp the stony roads carrying you in
our panting souls, our wounded love, our
desire to know the gentle nourishment
of the heaven you deeply loved. farewell,
dear friend, until we meet in that place
where the eternal ever so gently live.

THE VISION

I was walking along first avenue
having a kind of vision though not

you understand the sought you expect
from mystics and saints. I was living

in a building on whose rooftop the stars
appeared much bigger, then talking with

a group of friends while strolling along
avenue C. on the sidewalk beside the

empty lot growing flowers, I noticed
the pavement was littered with books,

old photographs, magazines, and a few
cracked ceramic Saints. a crowd began

to gather around the scattered items, kids
pointed at images in the photographs falling

over with laughter, a priest stopped to flip
through the pages of books tucking one

under his arm, a mother gathered up some
magazines placing them in a baby stroller,

then everyone disappeared without a trace.
when it happened, it grew quiet, my friends

too were gone, and I remained on the
corner only in the company of the cracked

figure of Saints. I looked around for any
sign of life, and my eye caught sight of a

feather gently falling to the hushed pavement.
I was convinced this must be a sign of some

kind though after all these years, the Loisaida
vision troubles me.

STRUGGLE

    we work, laugh, sing, dance, even
    look the other way with crosses hedging
    us in, forgetting Martin Luther King,
    Cesar Chavez, Oscar Romero, Rosa Parks,
    Fannie Lou Hammer are not streets. they
    lived from the start to speak to us of beginning
    dreams, to see kids grow free under their dark
    skin, know equality to breath the facts of
    democracy and claim this nation greater with
    their shapes. Black, White, Red, Yellow and
    Brown let the collective power of a righteous
    vision pound to imbue a future with greatness
    unbound.

THE GARDEN

at night, when the quiet drops,
I ask myself about the garden

where Jesus prayed for the cup
to be lifted, the hanging tree to

pass, a less tough heaven to come
to earth. with the slowly advancing

night, I cannot stop myself from
thinking about the Galilean who

was taken into death beside two
disarmed men who never called

him King. I wonder why divinity
made a show on the hill where blood

was spilled, followers fled, and women
wiped a body clean. up all night in

fragile light, I search the streets below
from my window for voices that will

tell me love left the garden for the lynching
tree to make a place for us in the rustling

dark chanting oblivion. I pull myself
together for a new day hoping to say

things unforgettable of the rabbi who
kneeled in a garden and waits in the

final twilight for us.

THE NAMELESS

I will tell you of the people who
speak loudly that no one cares to

understand, who experience their
days like a crime, and with shaking

heads wait for tenderness. I will walk
you down the street where holy Angel's

voices are mute, divinity has yet to offer
peace, and children who run the blocks

in play stop on the stoops to ponder
they are no more than luckless clay.

I will show you places in an ethically illiterate
world where the half-dead cry out for daily

bread in a flood of obscene days that are
neither seen or heard. I will ask you to

spend time among these sweet brown faces,
to bend your knees beside the angry, the

wounded, the sunken faced kids, the families
who stare at the graves of the dead, and the old

men and women whose eyes plead. I will
exhaust my life asking you to show slim

signs of care for the least of these.

STARRY NIGHT

tonight the city dark is new
with streetlights pointing the
way to the place the storefront
choir sings of things far beyond
itself. the light has never been
more clear for the mothers with
slender lips who live in shadows
that never speak, the nameless
around the block who find no reason
to believe, and those cut down for
whom we cry till Angel's wake.
tonight, Tito stopped to listen to
the choir sing earth's glory from
a dead street, airs of royal palaces
with marble stairs for tired feet, and
it made him shout: chévere!

HALLOWEEN NIGHT

on this Halloween the dark unveils
haunted apartments on every block,
with things tapping when kids come
close, ghosts that turn, twist and stare
in the dimly lighted halls, and shadows
spun into serpents by some unfathomed
mystery that makes them scream. in the
numbered flats of each tenement floor,
pots boil on the stoves with their own
brews of trouble made from chicken feet,
pigeon eggs, Crotona Park toads, tongue
of cow and feathers gathered from the sickly
Simpson Street tree. witches tell the kids to
chew the slowly cooking stews so the future
they will see, and frozen before each scary
door kids barely make themselves speak to
say trick or trick, that's all. trembling from
the knees on All Saints Eve, the kids from
the block with too many wronged days for
speech, feel on this invented night of fright
the strangest sense of glimmering light and
everlasting glee!

STICK BALL

we marked the street for the
Saturday morning stick ball

game, bases drawn with white
chalk borrowed from P.S. 118,

teams were picked to play the field,
the lookouts placed on the sidewalk

to call traffic, then hard breathing set
free to keep time. we used sticks from

thrown away brooms, and naked tennis
balls called by us the pink Spaulding. while

waiting in position for pinky to fly, we
thought of yesterday's school assembly

with an ex-baseball catcher who was ending
his days in a wheelchair, mothers who made

it home just ahead of the morning light, Hank
the wino who was always on the spot calling batter

up before his next little swig, little Victor on the
way to Viet Nam with the Marines, mild eyed

Rosa who left this world on a rooftop from
an heroin OD, Father Rossi who taught us

faith to deal with sin, and the future calling
from stones—stick ball we knew had a way

to pull the lessons together that entered our
heads.

THERE IS TIME

there is time to linger in the
church to watch the butterfly

scratch its back on the cross
above the altar, to talk with

the widows dressed in black
in the first pew with covered

heads, to listen to the Puerto
Rican girls talk about la Lupe

who can sing, and the street
that manages to slip us notes

with quality dreams. there is
time to walk down to Southern

Boulevard to mingle with the
old men who shine shoes, to

admire the Spanish speaking
movie house leaving neighbors

in a trance, to smell the flowers
lined on the sidewalk by the

old lady who could never afford
a shop, to listen to the Jewish

violinist sitting on a milk box in
the middle of the block playing

Albonini to brown skinned kids.
there is time to sit on stoops for

laughter, to take a hand to weep, to
picture other lives, and feel on this

bright day a pleasant vast peace.

TENDERNESS

the Angel comes in the simplicity of
night, the taxis drive beneath your

window blowing their horns, you hide
beneath sheets wondering about gods

who mysteriously human slept beneath
the stars in tents. the beating heart of

the city grows loud in your head this
night that appears to have no end with

the whispery Cherub propped against
the far wall of the room like a shadow.

in your mind you say dear presence why
have you come to this room whispering

things of another world your trembling ears
can barely hear? you think of your

mother who spends so many nights praying
to her Saints, a brother in the other bed

who stopped believing religious things, a
little sister who only wants to learn how

to whistle for the walk to church, and
the sea of harsh voices in the tenements on

your street. then, for no reason a few tears
commence to fall and your hear words said

with inexpressible tenderness, *do not be
afraid.*

WONDER

on the other side of Grand Concourse
in the shadow of a building with a medley

of Art deco curves, black granite, stainless
steel, and marble mosaic already on hard times,

boys and girls sit on the stoop with dreamy
eyes, talking. in a gentle breeze, a couple

holding hands walks past wearing smiles
scratched up to settle on their faces, and

from windows eyes accustomed to looking
at the sea take peaks at the crowded sidewalk,

the rolling buses, and the wrinkled faces of an
older generation, still. the kids conjure up

the future in English knocking hard at its tightly
shut door, switch to the Spanish spoken in the

parallel universe of their apartments, where mothers
and *Abuelas* practice intelligence by not speaking

a lick of the foreign tongue. on the other side
of Grand Concourse boys and girls sitting on

the stoop, gossip about mysteries half named,
then wonder why even the darkness treats them

like litter on the street?

ELECTION DAY

on choosing day,
the small voices
pounding
in every anxious
heart,
the world
keeping watch,
Washington, Lincoln
and the others lurking
in the atmosphere
like guards, comes
the moment to
decide.
on choosing day,
by the light of
Crucified Christ,
let ancient faith
in the ballot box
never be
denied.

THE POOR

in a neighborhood tucked
out of sight, hunger creeps

the alleys stalking families
everywhere met, mothers

stagger to church shouldering
despair, and the rich gather at

the edges of the city to feast
on finer things, ignorant.

when the wind begins to howl
in all directions on the block,

the poor start to wonder why
divinity has so much trouble

hearing the moaning in the
dark, the rising tide of doubt

about change, the hope there
was last week, gone now in the

morning light. the hungry here
who lived in many places have

felt water turned on them when
speaking of the enormous scarcity

of things that make a life. now,
they wonder about places offering

a piece of last light?

THE DAY AFTER

you asked me what the new day
brings, the pious times gone, the

shaken crowd captive of the dark,
human frailty cracked with whips,

people bent by hate, equal justice
coming undone, a sickening thug

for the President's place. you asked me
what comes next, I wondered out loud

how will the citizens step when they hear
the song, "When the Saints Go Marching

in," will they hobble for love or join
the goose-steppers shooting at us? you

asked me what will become of light, so
I looked into your eyes, invited you to

kneel, then we prayed to the keeper of peace,
the great High Priest, the beginning and end,

the battered and healed, the One nailed to a
tree who set us free, the impoverished Lord

who made the trampled rich, the murdered
human being who lives, to comfort us, and let

justice roll like waters now and righteousness
like an ever flowing stream.

THE STONE

today,
we woke
to democracy
wounded,
like something
drenched
in tears,
with voices
too frail
for words,
and eyes unable
to see dreams.
today,
we felt time
hobble
with the
saddest face
drifting
like dust
in spaces
of partial light,
and the
sobbing
did not
let our ears
hear
the future
shouting hope
from another
season.
today,
mysteries
like old maps
with clear
direction,
showed
up finally
to
move
the stone.

KINDNESS

when news of the election begins
to faint in newspapers carried by

another breeze and the people in the
fashionable houses begin to nod

goodbye to the country this use
to be before election day, what

will speak in your heads? when the
trampled of the earth invite us with

cries of woe to march with troubled
hearts, to lift them up with loving

arms, and turn away from the one
who makes the nation drift along in

flames, what spirit will stand beside
you in the dark? when the hardest

things of all come rolling from the
nation's house, the shredding of justice,

hope and love begins, the jails with
color filled, the others with wet eyes

calling, and the dream narrowed to
a tiny hint of White, what will pour

from your lips? Will you summon
the politics of peace that sings of justice

and knows the wounded are never
weak? will you hear the Word made

flesh singing on the streets: We shall
overcame!?

EVENING PRAYER

in darkest of hours, give us your peace.
in the bitter struggles for life, give us your Spirit.
in a world shouting hate, give us your love.
in every precinct of our wounded hearts, give us your touch.
in the movements for justice, give us your direction.
in the weight of things not understood, give us your wisdom.
in keeping company with the despised, give us your dreams.
in speaking to those with hardened hearts, give us your goodness.
in times we cannot find you, give us unlimited faith to see. Amen.

ELECTION DAY

how shall America
make history in
the bitter dark
to come, on
the Cross Christ
was nailed to
death, drifting like
an unanchored ship
away from freedom,
justice and the social
creed? what hearts shall
be disturbed by her weakened
unity, failing light, the
whispers here and there
of organized hate, and
the savage cries on
the streets and fields
of a dream took ill? how
shall we view the sun rise
over windblown trees, listen
to children play and wonder
why pale faces alone are
privileged to be free? how long
will we sit reflecting in the dark
about all the damage done and
the world gone on election day?
how long before we stand up to
tell him, my country, my country
tis not of thee!

IMAGINE

there is no perjury about
having little to look for in

life on these streets, everyday
a junkie dies alone in the dark

on the top flight of stairs leading
to a roof top spray painted with

names, old women who came
with pious fire from faraway just

talk of dreams suspended in time,
and suffering unchanged by their

praying minds. on this block, there
is no lying about churches that fled

the scene, the enormous arms of
the cops who beat us with thuggish

clubs until we bled, tears falling to
the ground yelling mercy all the way

down, and the dogged benediction
of the dark. imagine, there must be streets

with windows not greying, a place with
people who do not wish to be invulnerable

like the dead who now make speeches
from their graves, a corner of shared love,

unflinching reveries, and good that
happens from morning to night just for

us. wait and see, in that place, we will blithely shout and sing without end.

LETTER TO MY BROTHER

I have sat down once again to write this letter to you, Rudy.
I know you departed this world anonymously on a rainy Easter
Sunday night thirty-two years ago, but I hold on to the idea
that you are looking over my shoulder reading it.

My memories reach very far back to the day at the pre-school on
Long Fellow Avenue, when you put a gash above your right eyebrow
after a fall in the sandbox. I cried for you. We learned to see the world
with too much darkness, tears and pain playing on the streets in the South
Bronx.

Other people did not know how kind Victor's mother was to us
whenever food ran out at home for days, when she would have us
come by just to eat. She always tried with her sticky rice to put a
few more pounds on our flesh, and you never failed to smile at
her.

I cannot stop thinking about how the world did a great deal to
break your tender heart, bend you over its knee, then criminally
pound the sweet life from your pulsating veins. Mother and father
utterly helpless to prevent it, just ran away.   I go back often to a letter

dear to me written by James Baldwin to his nephew that reflected on
life in marginality in a world filled with racial hate that describes
the impossibility of being philosophical about enduring it. After your
departure, I can tell you with my own heavy-heart that Brown people
like us are no less loathed today, than on that night you unloved by
it passed away.

You know I was the foolish optimist who ran to Mass on Sunday, lighted
candles at the altar to Mary and the Saints, and naively prayed for love to
rattle the hearts of fellow Americans awake to a loving and broader common
good. After I buried you in Staten Island, and admitted God is nearer to
you now in this void opened in my soul,   I have continued with the foolishness
of love walking with those pounded into the ground for having Brown skin
and speaking another tongue.

Of course, for a very long time, and still now and then, I was convinced God had forgotten you existed, and when God finally looked you were already dead. I have
not changed too much Rudy, and still believe in the triumph of goodness in this pitiable world. Perhaps, you can understand that in a loveless world there is room for God's fools to engage in acts of kindness. I wish you had been given a little bit more life. I miss you, dear brother. Shalom! Harold

POVERTY

I saw an old apartment with a
cracked linoleum floor spread
across three rooms that was home
to the greatest living poor family
of the block known for crying on the
corners of the shopping district for
tiny pieces of bread. the family rich
with faith on the most wretched of its
hungry days carried stomachs filling
them with doubt. they waited in vain
for the downtown hearts to open with
concern, to see them unlock their doors
to let the split light of the pitiable rush the
dark, and for once call the wretched of
the earth by name. at night, I heard the
poor mother declare the kindness of others
was all she needed to turn hard times the
color of honey—imagine what divinity
must think of so much fading love, cracked
hope and the stinking world that easily takes
a leave from the hungry that poverty will
herd with many others into no more than
unremembered dust.

THE BIRTH

he was born on this land to
live in days that managed in
a thousand different ways
to shout at brown faces you
are not somebody. the people
around his immigrant kin who
survived in blistered tenements
without English names filled their
nights with stories of crossing the
hairline border into a new world that
breaks down dreams with hate. in the
city hospital where birth is bloody
his mother laid awake puzzling about
how to get a little more daily bread
and keep this earth and its religious
hypocrites from strangling her lovely
child's neck. he grew up to gather
friends with brittle bones on the corners
needing mercy, the kids who cried in
the barren fields of the block, and could
not find on the paths they trod a shining
light of bliss. he grew old holding others
by the hand, telling them to go on, pleading
for them to see way down the road, until they
find a place where the bitter storm clears!

THANKSGIVING DAY

it's thanksgiving day in my mother's
kitchen, I study the way she enters
the room holding a small brown bag

with seventy-five cents worth of herbs
to rub on a pork shoulder for the feast.
she moves around listening to the radio

until the remnant moon disappears,
shoving things in and out of the oven,
and dancing the time away with Latin

sounds coming from a transistor radio
on top of a small fridge. the radiator
in the room below the only window

chuckles at her steps, I smile by the
sink washing pans, and more secrets
from salsa king Tito Puente plays on

the transistor. while the pork roasted in
the oven, we talked of the Mayflower
Pilgrims who landed on a Northeast shore

with no trumpet blaring war, how the
first nations were murdered and robbed
clean, Africans for centuries held in

chains, a civil war to end with Black
humanity free, a nation with equality,
liberty, happiness, and badges shooting

spics. she faked interest in the conversation
and got real happy with the knock on the
apartment door that I was sent to answer

with my eleven year old sighs. friends
crowded into the apartment catching in wind
chilled noses the kitchen witchery my young

mother performed to simply give thanks for
friends, the blessed Mother of God, the fairy
spells conducted beneath an old mango tree,

the day she crossed the sea, and the new
linoleum carpet in the living room to be blessed
by dancing feet—Thanksgiving! Beautiful!

GOT IT

when we got to the church, petals
from Sunday flowers rested on

the steps, a woman with a sack
on the ground beside her wore a

faint smile on her freckled face,
a dog asleep in front of the apartment

building across the street sat up when
church bells began to ring, an old man

sitting with friends in the last pew called
to the young priest dashing down the aisle

more light, please. the dark bodies inside
brought to worship by exhaustion retreated

to thoughts about delighting heaven with
their needs, and the widows wearing black

scarves about their heads knelled at the
altar rail to demand from divinity above the

simple love to walk the naked streets once
more. when we got to the church, the cars

drove by with people laughing at our best
rags, and the Holy place we swore covered

herself with lighted candles to sob. the priest
who finally came to the altar astonished us

again with enchanting acts that only marched
us home after Mass with familiar silence.

COMMON GROUND

how do we search now for
common ground in the face
of the projections of ridiculous
hate, fears, broken community,
and divided citizen life? perhaps,
we will find it in the kindness that
transcends diversities, the inward
peace greater than our weaknesses,
the God within that has no need for
creeds, confessions, churches, or the
foolish talk of them, and the tender
acts of yielding ground to unbounded
love.

HUDSON HOTEL

I couldn't see in the light
from the bulb that dangled
at the end of a wire in a room

of a place that called itself a
hotel. the half-glass door with
shadowy movements passing

in front of it with loud shouts
penetrating the room assured my
anonymity in this world I was just

then coming to know. the place
was known to pimps, prostitutes,
felons, junkies, winos and lost boys

by the name Hudson Hotel. you could
escape the cold, ruined homes, knives
chasing you down the street, life

swinging from a thread for the simple
fee of $3.75 the night. whenever I
took a room to escape the cold the

lightbulb held my gaze in what seemed
to me a deep inexplicable silence like
the one I felt when Uncle Samuel died

on his farm in Jamaica that whispered
during the procession to the family plot
something I could not understand. often,

I could not sleep straight through the
night waking up to think about whether
or not my father's heart still pumped

to bring me home to the foot hills of
the Andes where he settled or whether
my siblings who prayed with blood on

their lips were slowly learning the
answers to things that would help them
find themselves. someday, the Hudson

Hotel haunting me I suspect will take
its leave and without the need to utter
a single word my soul will find peace.

WINGS

I wonder about the great wings of
Angels, the last time they rustled

above our heads, and sang to us in
the sweet hoarse voices of the departed.

who remembers? the women who
prayed in the corner church for

more than forty years, who never
tested priests with blasphemy, and

learned to rub their palms to make them
spread their wings like a curtain on a

stage with a big band behind it ready
to play even with the audience lights

out, remember. the Sunday school
teachers who had a fondness for talking

about Spirits hoovering about the block
beating their wings around us to make us

safe, remember. the kids who listened to
them like they were away at Summer camp

filled with unbearable homesickness, the
teachers' words worn like a charm around

their necks, remember. the people living
in heavy nights, feeling afraid, who weep

for you and me, remember.

FORDHAM ROAD

I found you standing on
Fordham Road staring at
the University. you said
that many years before you
studied at a school in another
language brought to Central
America from Spain. I walked
with you listening to the injuries,
secret fears, the crying that
you carry, and the loveliness
you believe passed away. we
lingered awhile on the corner,
watched the shoppers' doings
that busy morning, I held out
my hand attempting to charm
your troubles away, and meekly
we dared a prayer. your features
turned to smile, a taxi beeped
its horn at the two of us in stare,
and I promised to walk with you
until hearing the gentle hum that
comes with divinity near.

OLD CHURCH

there was a church on the Avenue
of the Americas where neighbors
from different parts of the world
once met to settle quarrels. But when
it turned one hundred years old on the
corner a final Mass was said to empty
pews with cobwebs hanging on them.
some people in the neighborhood tell
on certain nights they can still hear the
simple voices of celestial beings pouring
out on the sidewalk with songs of hope
and joy. others remember the days of
sending candid prayers to heaven from
the altar rail with bowed heads, the sounds
of sacred music reaching for the sophisticated
heights of the vaulted ceiling, and getting
ready for the dreamy chase of another day
of life. the building is still on the Avenue
converted to a nightclub visited now by
customers who understand the blood of
Christ and another round of gin are very
different things. But this old church on
the corner dismissed by priests and ignored
by theologians, on its floors with people now
doing spins, is still the sweetest mystery
you will see.

ANSWER

you look around
for a mouth to
speak a new edition
world in this
neighborhood
waiting for
it always on the
verge of
tears.
in the darkening
days you see the
uptown crowd ready
to clap for more
bars on the windows
and ankle chains for
people tongue-tied
in place.
you look around at
the aging mother's
with their world
to bear, who make
appointments at
Christmas and Easter
to converse with God
about matters of time
ignored by the clocks,
and ask questions
divinity does
not answer.
your eyes
rest in the
deepest silent
spots of the
block, again

you look around
for a mouth to
give answers
like the ones
in that tale they
say made
the wise men
weep.

WAITING

the light is coming on this
early morning slowly stirring

the street. the clear sky with
last night's stars still visible

fills workers with a feeling of
incomprehensible tranquility

while they walk to the subway
with the air thick of the smell

of incense that lingers on the
corner in front of a church. on

the wide avenue with the morning
slowly arranging itself Olga turns

to look back at her apartment where
she left two kids with sleep still in

their eyes dressed with orders to make
the long walk to school, quickly. by

the time she reaches the subway station,
walking past the bare branches of trees

in the little park, the kids carved with
Spanish names, she whispers to herself

in the prayed for light: I know a day
will come to lead us closer to the paths

our restless hearts and shivering limbs
long on this fractured block to walk.

BEND

across the street, in the
old building bending South,
the one lived in by Victor's
grandfather who likes to
sit on the stoop singing
themes from old Fellini
movies, where G.I. Manny
overdosed on a cold winter
night in the stairwell trying
to exercise the malignant
demon ordering him to war
in Vietnam, the place where
people crippled by hard work
retreat to complain in hushed
voices to their apartment walls
about petty wages, you can
close your eyes to feel an ocean
of dreams pour over you. I think
about that tenement nailed it seemed
to the sidewalk, filled with all kinds
of neighbors that wrapped life with
their views, and it occurs to me these
people standing on the promises of
love lived each day wondering what
would become of them. the night
curtain in that aging world of the
block has not yet fallen, on the stoop
these days you see faces returning to
this aching place from far off lands
with all kinds of good news to leave
darkness, undone.

THE PIER

at the end of the pier,
a little boy sits between
the legs of an old man,
looking silently out to
sea, an elderly woman
puts on a purple scarf
and stares at the water
inviting her collection of
memories, I borrow a
pencil from a backpack
teen just out of school,
to write myself a simple
note—"you know nothing
at all!" then, the darkness
creeping up, with beautiful
strangers everywhere, the
eyes on the pier look to the
passing moon that makes
them shine with a light so
ancient and clear that in that
magnificent instant sets us
finally free. what can be
more real?

PONDER

one day
the clocks
will chime
with the hour
we love most
delivering a message
for us
on these
shores
more precious
than all
the words
heard in the nearly
empty church.
there,
in the
mid-way to nowhere,
tossing life into
a godless wind,
we will
survive to hear it
and see the Lord's
rainbow lighting up
the sky.

EL BARRIO

I walked
around the
barrio,
passed the corner
young junkies
count the center
of the world,
their favorite
spot for
shouting at priests
holding Mass
on the church
steps,
and heard
the youngest mouth
holler: the meek inherit
nothing on these
streets.
an old woman
sitting on a stoop
on third avenue
reaping grace by
saying the rosary
shaking her head
told me the boy
doesn't have the
language right.
I paused in front of
Lela's building
looking up
at her apartment
where the gas
was cut off
and asked
myself
why the Lord
made this night
so very, very
long?

SIMPLE

the scene changed when
I saw a cheerful squirrel

run up a tree reaching for
the heights of heaven just

when the clock began to
ring. I saw a man coughing

walking a chubby German
Shepherd that never ran a

mile, the sky still burning
last night's stars, and the trees

unclothed of leaves no longer
able to speak with the breeze. the

world was once simple enough
to fit in this small space, easy to

describe completely alive on the
street, and plainly comprehended

like old prayers taught in bible class
echoing ancient truths. I suspect

there are simple views of the world
working overtime elsewhere, places

not full of bitter weeping, people not
pining for love, and luxuriously varied

faces like flowers hiding insights too
deep for words. But, for now, in the

grasp of wonder offered by the playful
little creature that ran up a tree, I bend

my ear to listen for an answer that some
morning will turn toward me, and I will

roam in it blissfully free.

THE BIG TREE

near the big green Christmas
tree at the center of town, when

the stars shined bright and joy leaped
from darkness, I met a beggar who

trembled from the cold named
Hank. his old eyes were lovelier

than the holiest of dreams, they
marveled yearlong at ordinary

trees, and the fresh truth of living
on the street. he regularly came out

on evenings vainly waiting for wild
bells to ring in the stone hearts of the

visitors viewing the tree, for anyone
to give their jacket, hat and scarf

to drive his shivering away, but no
one ever saw old Hank. I listened

uttering heresies about gracious love,
wrapped my arms around the beggar,

my Christ, and gave him my coat. then,
with a weakening faith I prayed for this

stumbling world to see in Hank Jesus the
King—and make things new!

HERE

I move in a world
roaming around with
people whose hearts
are sometimes too
cramped with complaints
for God.
I have huddled
in their apartments listening
to young mothers with children
asleep in their laps
who wondered out loud
why so much time
is spent talking
about divinity
found in a
book—words
are full of
lies
they say.
I have learned
how they
live in a world of
screams, hide what
they think of priests,
and quietly turn to
bone.
I have listened
to thoughts tumbling in
thinly furnished living rooms
unable to explain the endless
feeling of getting
nowhere.
I have been
kissed and treated
with kindness by those
below who long to
live—and here I
will remain.

CHRISTMAS, ROCKEFELLER CENTER

with the wordless infant in mind
I was brought to my knees one
night at Rockefeller Center, after

riding the subway for hours to stay
out of the cold, where I finished off
a piece of day old buttered bread the

Valencia Bakery clerk gave me with
Christmas cheer. I had never seen
so many people finely dressed who

had never gone hungry in one place,
their eyes spinning all over the piazza,
naked cameras flashing the whole night

beside the tree, by the ice rink, and at
the open mouths on the steps of Saint
Patrick's Cathedral. I felt peace standing

where the lights were on, imagining myself
with a home, enchanted by the sounds of
the season, and tossed to the top of the

huge tree, awake. I thought it would be
so natural from that height to look at the
flat world to say the stench of the stable

is just around the corner in the dark you
do not see, the bodies of the bums beneath
cardboard asleep, the girls bickering over

johns, and the injured expressions marking
the faces of throwaway kids. on that cold
homeless night, I hummed *Go Tell It on the*

Mountain, listened to the visitors talk in
different tongues, and heard children sweetly
sing. I wanted so much to believe, but in

the homeless cold, I found myself instead
cursing the Holy silence.

REDEMPTION

on the street, in the cold
winter, steering around
for places with heat, the
mind imagining the smell
of warm apartments, leads
the heart to sob. the churches
terrified at your sight and repulsed
by your filth hardly ever have
an open door during the bitter
freezing weeks. trembling no
matter where, the citizens think you
criminal not a person beat down
with nothing to your name, even
the tears streaming dirt down
your face is out of sight for most
of them. on the street, you dream
someday the homeless frail will
be counted, along with all those
who died from the cold, and lastly
redeemed.

PIETY

       one night the kids on
       the stoop, sitting with
       their first bottle of Colt
       45 Malt liquor, began
       showing the scars nobody
       had ever seen. they talked
       about them like one would
       an old shirt with holes on
       the elbows they were forced
       to wear to school. they passed
       the quart bottle around saying
       they were never really able to
       bury the beating days, the fake
       saints on the home altars could
       not stop. Lefty from the other
       block broke down when he lifted
       his shirt to show a back full of
       scars that no one with smoother
       skin ever suspected. these kids
       who stopped believing in Angels
       and could not stand feeling helpless,
       drank. when Lefty got his hands on
       the bottle again, he poured a little beer
       on the ground saying, for the dead, the
       dying and kids beaten in those damn
       pious homes. when the bottle was
       nearly finished, Shorty, a seasoned altar
       boy schooled by nuns, cried out the only
       thing the Colt 45 needed was a little bit
       of altar bread to make the night complete.

THE MUSICIAN

the morning, looked up
colored yellow by the
sun, while the elderly
musician set up a spot
in the alley between two
buildings to play. the old
performer who held us
in his hands bowed his
violin to pass on sounds
that sweetened the start of
another day with enchanting
pitches made of the purest milk and
honey. he lifted sadness to the
clouds, put sky wide smiles on
the faces at open windows, and
almost mended the broken hearts
that cried at the first sign of the
blowing Southern wind. when the music
was done, the people at the windows
dropped change wrapped in old newspapers,
or placed in small brown bags. they clapped
for the old musician to thank him for luring
their hearts to places thought lost.

PEACE

    the story-tellers will stay up
    into the dark night sitting on
    the linoleum floors, pointing
    to loud trumpets blowing with
    simple words, talking about an
    infant Lord with a sweet dark
    face, born in a foul stable, and
    rich with grace. their wide-eyes
    will declare to people who live
    afraid, find the newborn swathed
    in heavenly love, especially on your
    knees. the story-tellers tonight will
    spin tales from once upon a time, in
    a land far away, years and years ago,
    unto us a child was given, the Prince
    of Peace, the one who scatters the proud,
    raises the lowly and beats old Herod at his
    cruel games. the story-tellers will be
    up tonight with manger news of light
    that leaves nothing in the world the
    same—Alelujah, Gloria a Dios!

THE DROP

the moon,
drops light to the
street
and Hector
already on the stoop is
still, listening.
the tranquil
dawn raises him above
unkind strife where his
knotted throat
learns to part the dark
like a flashlight in a
cave.
on that day,
he was convinced
God was talking
to him of his favorite bible
passages,
breathing words
into his ear, gently telling
him not to forget
on these shores his
Spanish name will always
give him away.
he reached
for a tiny stone
resting on the steps,
placed it in the palm
of his cracked hands,
thought
of the gravestones
in the cemetery down
the street he often
called roots for

the people on
the block, then
sighed
amen.

THE GUITAR

the guitar came out
at ten playing songs
for the gathered about
distant things, time spent
in other territories hugged
by tearful clouds, night
talk of keys turned after
work in rusted tenement locks
and crushed letters from lovers
over the border carefully stored
in American shoe boxes. the guitar
played wrenching blues far into the
night, in brown hands it moaned
about troubling things in broken
English souls, the walls of Jericho
not down, and longings for what
no one any longer could recall. the
guitar played, its six strings never
hearing silence, and it sang us into
a gentle weep.

FALSE ARREST

on the way to the apartment
a long way from the block,

we talked about the cops who
breathed on the back of Tito's

neck, you have the right to remain
silent, nothing should come out of

your mouth, we don't want to hear
about your diabetic mother, or fall

down dead brother, or that Father
Rossi will burst through his grave

to speak of your innocence, tonight.
Spic, next time you see us coming

you best run. shaking our heads about
how Tito was framed by a dropped bag

of dope found on the sidewalk by his
feet, we whispered can you believe

it, the face of the man is white and
they keep telling us God is too. walking

a little faster, we laughed thinking out
loud that explains why our prayers are

never answered. we finally got to the
apartment, walked quietly pass the altar

with Brown faced Saints, a Black Jesus
and an Indian Chief, and whispered all

we need is for Ezekiel to take us by the
elbow, while speaking to this valley of dry

bones of better days coming for God's
dark people.

THE MOTHER

I left you eight books,
a pair of blue jeans, a
polka dot shirt, a notebook
full of scribbles, and my
cherished childhood. I
left a note between the
sofa cushions describing
the scent of Orchard Beach,
the food you gave us there to
eat, the music stand in my
little sisters room still saying
farewell, and my shadow that
fell on the linoleum floor. my
next note will be pushed to you
by an envelope from an abandoned
building with splintered floors, exiled
bricks, broken chairs and homeless
kids. read it with blood-shot eyes,
feel the dust on your skin, and though
you threw us away hope for us and
think now and then of our names.

NEW YEAR

tonight, the old year will
leave not a trace just seconds
after midnight, all talk of
yesterday will be gone come
Spring, the past year's hopes
will be laid in new ground to
learn from the ashes of what
is put to rest. tonight, a new
year will begin to lead us to
fresh truths to spread from
the rooftops from boxes filled
with paper airplanes with words
to toss into the coming new time.
tonight, we will wonder in the
new year of those with full stomachs
who speak to others with nothing
to eat and the slanted politicians
who spread filth they name justice,
unity and peace. tonight, after
a thousand steps taken in the dark,
with half prayers, we will face what
comes and never disappear.

AFTER SCHOOL

In the Fall, on Wednesday
they let us out of school early

to meet with Father Rossi for
religious instructions. what was

experienced most ours was the
long walk to the church office

rehearsing the things we really
believed like showing up to the

priest's office late, or feeling the
warm sun on our quivering lips

when reading walls with good
news scribbled in graffiti, or

holding our noses to keep from
smelling Hank's hobo stench

on the stoop and wondering on
the way to catechism what God

had against him. just once, we
wanted Father Rossi to come to

us walking at night, find us on
the stoops debating the future

louder than fuming drunks, in
the apartments where mothers

are eager to tell their own true
stories and children never have

enough to eat. just once, we
wanted the catechism giver to

come into a world where religion
finally turns to dust and even the

little kids looking behind them say
good bye sweet Lord skipping away.

just once, on the edge of the
afternoon, we wanted to attend

the after school religious instruction
class with Father Rossi, pull from

our cheap trouser pockets globs of
playdough, make an image of God,

and wait to hear what the good priest
had to say of the universe crawling in

it.

WHERE

what is astonishing about this
night is the complicated details
of love, dreamier than all the
wandering stars, in the heart
commanding, intently sketching
a million places to find the deepest
colors of the soul, luring us from
room to room, way beyond the rules
of knowledge, far from all the grieving
tongues, and to the hidden spaces of
sugary peace.

COLD

somehow,
the world manages to
go around the cold that
shakes you more on these
streets than I can remember.

somehow,
you use your smile to hide
a body almost turning blue
in the icy wind you say each winter
is on bad terms with God.

somehow,
the winter's jagged edge finds
a way in through your barricade of
old clothes, insensitive to prayers,
and impartial to your unpolished name.

somehow,
above the ground another day
far from the blasting furnaces,
with a hoarse voice you say lets
go to the candlelight at the church.

somehow,
I want to believe there is a
miracle to find in it, like the
swallowed wafer that warms,
while everything else in the

world remains in a cold
season.

¡AY, BENDITO!

speaking Spanglish the day long,
to announce Brown dreams waking
heaven on earth, making perfect two
tongued sounds that follow rules of
sense in Spanish, English and double-talk
slang makes mundos once apart mass together
for a chévere naughty dance. come see the
out loud intelligence of our non-standard
speech, the world conjured by our talk of
los muertos, the Santos that hang on our
necks, Diosito who digs our stoops and the
bodies aqui tangled full of life made from
ancestral Red, African depths and an Iberian
tinge. ¡Ay bendito, que gente! en este lugar,
the congas play the weekends into the dark
night, people lean into their ancient sounds, the
wind blows in all four directions, and we smile
for the wise mysteries to wander in. ¡Ay bendito,
que gente! come see this world turn, make a
chapel in your heart, listen on the streets for love,
and head with us to the place where fear always
comes undone.

LOST DAY

I am looking for a day carelessly
lost in time one aged wet afternoon
on Tremont Street. The cross town
bus went by on it with signs painted
by poverty and clocks telling time
full of inviting things. I called the
public transportation dispatch office
to inquire whether or not the lost and
found department had any piece of this
day turned in, but they evaded my inquiry
with disturbed eyes. without pause, I
roamed the neighborhood where people
only own the clothing on their backs,
stopped at the Botanica to talk with the
sorcerers about how that day vanished
like the sugarcane we use to eat, the ocean
that bathed us clean, and the island that once
gave us coconuts to drink. Looking down the years,
I hope to find that day before it's too late, and
see kids on the block walk in it for a long while
in the gladness dreadful timepieces dare not
touch.

RAIN

when it rains the children fear
the sky is falling, grandmothers

believe water drops are the tears
of the dead, and old tired men with

huge smiles wait with open mouths
to drink. with eyes closed you can

listen to the different ways the wild
rain falls, the plunk of heavy drops

hitting the sidewalks, and the ancient
pouring of earth's first days offered

up now for play. in the apartment
next door, Carmen Julia is singing

her dearest songs happy to feel at
rest in a world where no one else has

lived, rescuing from the folds of her
deepest memories bliss from the years

that settled inside her like dust. we believe
the power coming from the clouds of a

curved sky washes us with the sighs of
the blowing wet wind, clean.

FLIGHT

the time was talked about for
weeks, the mountain passes

to walk covered by the dark
sky, the hills spotted by the

white dressed middle aged
men carrying coffee sacks on

their backs to scale in the valley.
I heard you think loud enough to

shake leaves saying you will come
back to drink café someday in that

quiet dell, after years of cleaning
houses with many tears to waste

your cheeks, months of dreaming
sweet blessings on the children in

your keep, and days attached to the
feeling of better times to come. I saw

your frail hands tremble before the sight
of the little village called home the moment

it began fading in the dawn mist, your
garments were then soiled by the long

walk, and I became aware the wrong
causing your flight belongs to a country

not of thee. when a branch swept across
your face, you paused to take a deep breath,

gently pushed it behind you, then
smiled to tell me the landscape will not

change. as we walked past a bomb-outed
building, I held your hand, we stopped

and closed our eyes, then listened to God's
birds singing without intermission from the

tree tops—soon, and very soon like the
song says!

THE CLIMB

I think about the beautiful mornings
on the stoop just when school let out

for Summer, the long memories of the
old Jewish watch repair man who would

place a beach chair on the sidewalk to
catch the murmurs of the young Puerto

Rican mothers strolling baby carriages
down the avenue. I can see Manolo home

on leave wearing Marine dress blues with
blood stripes running down the trouser legs,

and a hat all the kids thought sure was white
with an eagle, globe and anchor looking like

it was hoisted into place, and Manny though
fallen never forgotten on the roll call of the

block for keeping Brown bodies free. I
remember how Tony would take popsicle

sticks to toss them in water flowing like a
stream from an open fire hydrant standing

in the middle of the block, chasing them
with his drumming heart along Westchester

Avenue like they were somehow leading him
to a door where lost dear ones would be sitting

in wait. hush, sweet friend, I feel these itinerant
memories indifferent to sadness make me firmly

wish for more beautiful summer mornings like
this to climb.

SOUND

the nightly conversation
sparkled with brilliance in
that little crowded room,
where you slowly dried your
eyes with words used to paste
stories together full of warmth.
I remember the glad mood they
put in the bedroom to pull us into
our own fifth floor Neverland with
all the astonishing things imagination
believed. you know, since you've
been gone, I have more than once
demanded to speak to God in person
with no real success. I suppose you
already know that last night, I walked
the last flight of steps to the roof to
once again request an audience with
the unmoved above. I waited a long time
in the silence, then shouted anyway to
heaven that I can't remember the sound
of your sweet voice—for some reason it
just won't come!

THE WAY

history will decide
what of America is
in the Trump face,
the voices to wake
Abe Lincoln from
the grave, the pen
that turned refugees
away, the clatter of
plowshares turned to
swords, the wealth of
a cabinet knitted from
the poor and measures
to make this land less
free. history will decide
what dream was lived,
the scars worn, and the
way to make America,
again!

THE STAND

each,
new day begins
with the luminous clarity of
fear,
in all the places
the strangers from another
shore
see justice
dissolve into a
deep and mute
well.
the undocumented
lady who lives on
the fifth floor
of the corner building
says in daylight the
miracles
no longer come
and no matter how
beautiful the
sky appears above
her head
darkness has
become the
appearance
of things.
each,
new day the
air shrieks at the sight
of the hand of unbearable
power
that is tallying
the numbers of those
who must bleed to
satisfy
the hate swarming
like flies around the
white in their
leader's eyes.
each,
new day those
who love strangers
with another
sense,
will stand
with the beautiful
deeply known to recover
every discarded
life.

KNOCK

I walked along the avenue
knocking on store windows,
remembering how the kids
that watched each other cry
always played this game to
hide sadness. I looked at people
inside the shops with worn faces
appearing like they had spent too
many nights feeling around in the
dark, I thought about all the kids
on the block who go on dying, and
then managed to smile at the old man
in the pizza shop who tenderly put his
arms around the first child in the
restaurant who started to leave. again, I
knocked on the window only this time
looking directly at the elderly man, I
whispered, *run slow sweet love until
the hurt on this forgotten block is spent.*
I went up the street, entered the sanctuary
of the only open church, lit a candle with
no particular prayer lunging into space
from my lips, and an old priest took my
hand to offer a blessing. on the way out
of the sacred space, walking past the
confessional box, I knocked on its little
window to see who would pop out of
that dark and narrow place.

HUNTS POINT

that day I went with Joseph
to Hunts Point shipping yard
there was tall grass, sky reaching
trees and a waterfront noisy with
whispers, telling me what I needed to
know about endless mystery. with the
stars still twinkling above on that early
morning, I confess never imagining
blocks away from the neighborhood we
called home a moment would so carefully
arise to offer us luxurious feelings of peace.
my eyes wetter than the sea in front of
them promised with every sight they
drew in the sweetest joy that I swore
to carry back to the block, to walk it
around the streets, and on the rooftop
with an invitation to God---come down
and see! after years of growing up, I
hear Hunts Point still calling my name
bidding me never to say farewell. so,
I carry that place within looking toward
the future like nothing less than a perfect
Nazareth dream.

EXIT

the rocks,
cry to us alarmed
by the things decided
in the office of a sorry
politician belching public
policy that bruises justice
with an unimaginable new
prison.

the stones,
scream beneath
our feet about trampled lives
with no place left to rest in a
country with a perfect love
for a cracked liberty
bell.

the rooftops,
fill these days with the
footprints of the innocent
who nightly visit to drop
leaflets describing for the
world the White House sorcery
that makes the common good
a smug story of unshared
love.

broken hearts,
in thick suffering recall blessings
from beyond, good news from above,
messengers of kindness, sacred signs
from the earth, nourishing words of peace,
the revelations the seers see, and in the
brutal season the gods still touching them
with grace!

LAMENT

I am sitting here beside
you the door tightly shut
tears falling to the table
top in a room where the
sound of laughter has all
but nearly gone. you already
damaged by the ritualized hate
grasping the country by the
neck are threatened yet again
with crucifixion. I pour coffee
into the Mexican made cup your
American born daughter gave you
four birthdays ago, you sigh the
story of crossing several borders
of suffering and death, to come to
this land you hoped would let you
dream life fresh. you hold a piece
of morning bread to offer that partly
crumbles to the kitchen floor from
your shaking hand, the knot in my
throat cannot find a single word of
praise for the gracious Being that
imagined us, differently. we have
lived in the shadow of death for so
long, crept around cemeteries
here and there, roamed the places
where Jesus wept, and raised the
same question again and again to
heaven above—why have you
forsaken us? yet, in a strange way,
we fall to our knees in your tiny kitchen
crying one more prayer with tongues
burdened by the thought that joy will
not come in the morning, and still giving
in to the loving arms of the divine.

AWAKE

    awake in the common light,
    democracy shredded by
    the terrifying new reality of vain
    ignorance with might, an old racist,
    open misogynist, morally failing
    president stomps the White House
    Halls. in this colossal dim light we
    do not despair, scatter like troubled
    dust, and truth unclearly see!

THIS TIME

the darkness
around us in this
aching land
will
never find
a place
to settle
in our shouting
dreams.
the years
to come will
answer for the deeds
signed
against Eden
and all the
better gods
to please the
fuddled knowledge
of a brutish head of
state.
our hearts
even now
lift to
paradise
with the knowledge
that history
is poorly made
by
abysmal power
and
politicians
with so much
stamina to
fail.

one day
not far, we
will
sing together
carrying the corpse
of these
misdeeds to the
edge of the earth
and
dropping it
into a perfect
sulfurous
hell

LENT

lent in silence begins to say
we are ashes turning to dust,
light for darkness, and proud
marchers to Calvary. even the
salt in falling tears is offered up
for sacrifice in the thickening
forty days. lent speaks to us of
a God who dies to mark us with
the glorious coordinates of true
life. and now, in this new season
of nothing ever lasts, far from the
bantering talk that gathers the
makers of the Cross who require
more departed, we are not afraid
of death knocking at the door, hate
turning the world mad and those
unaware of how justice agonized
on the crude hard wood of the cross
does sweetly gather for us!

ROADSIDE

all day the sun shines
above the top of a mountain

for time that began with
people on foot for miles to

find work that never comes.
the local priest wakes into the

warmth of morning with rituals that
pass on the sacramental love giving

life to bony-waisted kids stomping
their way to a school with too few

books for eager lessons. I sit on
a stump beside the road leading to

Morazán wondering out loud when
heaven will dip down on the valley

to drop its light on us, to deliver
everyone from fear, and ease us

into restful night. an old school
bus sent from the United States

crawls up the craggy road, when
the smell of its exhaust is cleared

by the gentle breeze, I breath
deeply the earth's Spring and

hum louder than anyone cares
to hear the sweet signs of adored

and innocent life in these hills.

BELOVED COMMUNITY

when strolling alone
outside to see the stars,
I wonder how to speak
in a world broken by
contempt, the words
lunging to the tip of my
stuttering tongue, do not
take away the bread that
gives sweet life. along time
ago in a world the length of
the blue sky we easily imagine
is touched by ageless love, I
felt the warm affection of men
and women with passion for
the poor, warmth for dark
hands, dreams enough for
everyone on this ancient and
consecrated earth. no matter
the stony path we pace, the
slippery bends beckoning us
in the world to hate, lets ascend
to the mountain top with torn
and joyful hearts to let beloved
community claim us like the
great moment life graciously in
time appeared.

.

WHAT MATTERS

the politician
who has never
felt the weight of a
poor souls shoes,
dribbling ignorance
from an idle mind
with obscene
villainies to toss,
will never
understand
the love arising
in us that marches
on the streets
chiseling in the
frightened
and mournful
eyes a will
to make heaven
on this darkening
earth.
before too
long the stifling
announcements
this well dressed
thug creates, which
make us heave
sighs and heaven weep,
will drop on the
world's ears transparent
like a bucket full of
lies.
you see,
the misfit politician
cannot keep us from
fetching
candles to flame in
the dark where
justice lingers to
swallow
malefactors
like him
who make frail
hearts break.

BREAD

in the evening with a breeze
blowing across the mountain

peaks teasing a fresh new day
to make all the shadows fade,

I recall the man who walked
barefooted with wood across

his shoulders found on the side
of the road beside soldiers who

roamed the hills perishing with
a violence that coughed from

swallowing so many of them
up. the man scavenged land turned

by civil war to ashes, he talked of
the nameless poor bent with tears

behind coffins, and exhausted
from years of never being noted.

yesterday, I ate bread made by his
hands, confessed this food the world

should eat, and prayed the meek of
the earth like him threatened by the

grave should receive from heaven
their resurrection long before turning

to simple dust to fill the stony paths
of earth.

SIMPLE WOOD

there is nothing left to
worship save the cross

that hangs on string around
our necks made from simple

wood pressed with the brightest
colors. we take it everywhere

the great worry builds a home,
the halls of scientific inquiry, the

places where soldiers live, into the
life-bleeding courts, the unsacred

spaces where priests are exceedingly
unfree, and to the strangers hearing the

ungainly sophistry of a world gone
real mad. we need no lights to see by,

save the tiny cross with us in the
tightest wind, wherever the shovels

turning earth for us ring, to dream
a different spell of life will blow in

with copious milk and honey. there
is nothing left to worship in places

where the wretched mourning of
the poor is shunned by those who

aim to please. there is nothing
left to worship, save the cross made

like us from dust that we expect
will purify the blankest soul with

love.

FISH PLATTER

that first trip to City Island
with my mother in a sky blue
1961 Thunderbird was a day

of mystery—I had no idea she
was so fond of the little place
with a whole bunch of Puerto

Rican short order cooks tossing
plates of fish. when we got there
it was almost dark, people once

from villages on another island
out to sea speaking only Spanish
smiled together, while eating the

foreign language catch taking on
light on their plates. I ate a platter
of shrimp for the first time in my

eleven years, looked into my mother's
brown eyes, she giggled, I realized
happiness comes on slowly. it occurred

to me the same wind blowing through
the apartment windows, caressing the
nearly bald heads of the *viejos* who played

dominos more than prayed, the one
trembling to the top of the church steps
making widows bow their heads, passed

over us. we left that fish paradise carrying
our mute souls back to a tenement mother
never called home, on the long ride, I pled

for a different wind to take us to a place that
offered a glimpse of something that says this
is how you live.

THE OTHER SIDE

on the other side of High Bridge
the world was having a different

kind of dream that belonged to
those who never crossed the East

River. some afternoons we walked
half way across it to shout into the

cross winds stories about the aching
streets, the abandoned schools, the

desolate churches, and the weeping
mothers who tried too late to circle

their kids. on streets over there
English tongues talk threats with no

regard for how falsely they describe
us in their rounded world. from the

distance, we easily see a big old
church whose symbols do not

speak of Spanish strangers' faces
with depth and light for anyone

willing to cross the distance. I
traversed the bridge alone one early

summer morning convinced the rules
that divide English lives from Spanish

terrain on this same earth needed
to be reordered in time and space

and imagined over, again.

THE TRUMPET BLOWS

at the border, the guards
cannot see the line acting

like a locked door to keep your
face out. the gatekeepers, paid

to eye you have overlooked the
story of a simple stick in a fear

gripped hand that split the Red
Sea to make a way for the newly

free that no bitter law reached. at the
border, in dark and light where you

regard the memory of the murderers
you flee, the grotesque scientifically

imagined fence, hatched in the appalling
inner space of a leader with down turned

lips will in American time not even yelping
dogs restrain. at the border, once this cursed

wall is complete the long light that led you
all this way shall light all its parapets, while

the Jericho trumpets blow sweet crumbling
hymns. at the border, on that heavenly day,

you will whisper into the barrier cracks the
wailing prayers those people on the other side

have forgotten to say and hear.

POURING RAIN

the rain poured down from
rooftops one afternoon that

greeted the sadly-widened
eyes of kids who played on

a stoop tossing pennies. they
left without a trace in search

of another Eden that they
believed could be found in

the hallway of building 1203,
where old men often gathered

at night to spill years of living
into rum cups. their joys here

at the bottom of the world had
the warmest touch and the simple

mysteries of life brushed their
hearts more deeply than all the

rows of logic learned at school
that pretended to explain a poor

barrio life. these kids have never
laid in a daisy field to look up

at clouds, slept in a bedroom in
a big old house, wheeled bikes

dangerously down thickly green
summer streets, or remembered

books about Jack and Jill going up
a hill to fetch water. these young

Brown kids tossed like leaves in a
storm adored nothing more than

standing in each other's light.

THE BOYS

    they walked down the sidewalk
    almost in each other's arms joking
    about what was said in the Saturday
    night confessional booth to the priest
    who was just appointed to serve the
    Hoe Avenue church. one boy held
    a small brown bag in his left hand
    from the corner bodega that contained
    twenty-five cents worth of six whole
    leaves of *recao* requested by his grandmother
    for the mix of spices required to flavor an
    evening meal. the two boys appeared happy
    in the feinting light, untouched by any trouble
    lurking in the shadows, distanced from threats
    made by the figure of death always seeking to
    enter their lives with a speech. these boys
    simply walked in happiness for anyone who
    cared to stand to the side, and see.

THE STOOP

    the thin girls,
    holding flowers and
    making music on the stoop
    with voices pushing
    sounds from
    within to make their heavy
    world light
    belong on a Spring city stage
    with the wakeful Sun urging us to
    dance around them.
    creation sings
    with them every afternoon
    to make the passersby spill secrets
    on the stoop,
    rumors of a sinless world
    and
    curses for those who too
    quickly forget the simplicity
    of dreams.
    the thin girls,
    many like to say know
    the meanings invented
    by nuns who first offered
    bread,
    talked to them of
    Saints,
    and with their fingers
    always pointed to
    the stars in boundless space.
    the thin girls,
    on the stoop who sing
    of life's necessities, so the
    old folks say are candles
    that will never blow
    out.

SAY!

What can I say in this dismal
season of alarming politicians
so travelled by hate? What can I
say of the meek who mourn? Who
are they who bless these days with
tears? my tongue will shout their
names, my prayers call out to their
graves, and the language of the
governors that make these shores
dark, will with God I pledge fall
quickly to dust!

GRADUATION

rather,
sooner than
expected
the world has
grown you
straight up.
we will set
the table for
four
but with
the last moon
of summer,
with all your
questions college
will step out of
the night to
kindly draw
you in.
soon,
send off day
will take me
to the place
of tears,
but you
already know
I promised to dry
these fatherly eyes
as quietly as the
the great springs
of knowledge
welcoming
you will
flow.
soon,
when you
shine your
light on campus,
I suspect floating
miracles will in
you find a new place
to come for
rest.

CLOTHESLINE

scrawny pigeons were balanced
on clotheslines in the alley growing

thinner by the seconds, waiting for
a piece of bread to be thrown from

a window to the concrete below them
from the hands of another hungry

resident of the block. these pigeons
were in the habit of looking down to

the earth that unconsciously had forgotten
to provide them with tiny bits to eat. young

Puerto Rican mothers opened windows to
let time move through their apartments, they

leaned over window sills hanging expensive
things on the lines that adorned ordinary days

with a charmed odd glow. we played beneath
these dangling rags making up our lived world,

running around with wildly cursing tongues,
looser than the paper-thin walls in our homes.

sometimes, we lined up below the ravenous
birds on the line imagining those freshening

clothes with memories, aware the block kept
nothing from us, and soon the drying rags

would cradle our bones back to school, play
or work, where we listened for the ring of a

cool stillness.

BUS RIDE

on the bus ride down
the giant avenue, I could

see people sitting on the
stoops wearing smiles to

cast aside the many days,
weeks, months and years

colored by sadness. quietly,
I looked around the transit

carriage packed that afternoon
with our midway to nowhere

souls imagining that before
the next stop someone would

reach into a pocket to pull out
an immense blanket to wrap

around our drooping shoulders
with the kind warmth that brings

an end to glassy stares. the bus
flew past the Catholic church

with a stature of Saint Anthony
on the bottom step of the main

entrance door, and I could see
someone placed flowers at his

feet, along with a bowl of fruit
no doubt he happily ate in the

darkest part of night, when no
one was looking. the sparrows

from another land winged past
the front windshield of the bus

startling the old Black driver
who knew many passengers

by name. abruptly, the corner
where grown men shined shoes

came into view like candles at
the edge of life. I saw Hector

in his typical first one on the
boulevard spot talking to a

couple of little Nuyorican kids
no doubt of the African, Iberian

and Indian in their skin, and
remembered all the lessons from

his tell you everything lips. in
the middle of the block a group

of grandmothers who use to
ride the subway downtown to

stitch and sew in a building
bleeding clothes they could

never afford to wear, came out
of a tiny market with shopping

bags piled high with rice and
red beans. they were heading

back to the apartments to prepare
these things in homes hungry for

God to rain new dreams.

MR. PRESIDENT

> the world is coming undone,
> the unbearable wounds of
> the nation remarked by the
> news in the language of ruin,
> the existence of it flashes like
> a neon sign at night the word,
> slime. woe to those who do not
> give a damn, who raise banners
> of hate, who seek the pallid empire
> that makes this life a waste. Sad.
> before too long they will all say
> what have we done, why did we
> work so hard to dissolve the best
> idea that came many years ago in
> waves: out of many One. Woe
> to those who forget democracy
> is worthless tomorrow, unless it
> shines today.

www.ingramcontent.com/pod-product-compliance
Lightning Source LLC
Chambersburg PA
CBHW050827160426
43192CB00010B/1925